Detective Zoro

Book 2

Legend of the Drowned City

With Best wishes!

Hello Reader,

Col. Zoro is on vacation. Wait, hang on a minute – a real detective, soldier at that, is NEVER on vacation!!! Col. Zoro realizes this the hard way as he heads on a well – earned holiday after solving the mystery of the haunted lake. Even before his vacation starts, he is caught up in a sinister web, carefully laid out by the enemy!

To tell you the truth though, Col. Zoro thoroughly enjoys adventures and challenges. So, dive right in and I hope you enjoy reading about his adventure as much as he did, living it!

From,
The Author.

that, Col. Zoro?" he asked,
g with a big suitcase.

at?" asked Col. Zoro in **surprise**,
s hand bag. Just then, he glanced
what Wodi was pointing.

as a scrap of paper sticking out
s pocket. 'I wonder what this is now,'
ed thoughtfully.

ewspaper cuttings
asted all over the paper when he
ed it.

ormed a **CHILLING** message.

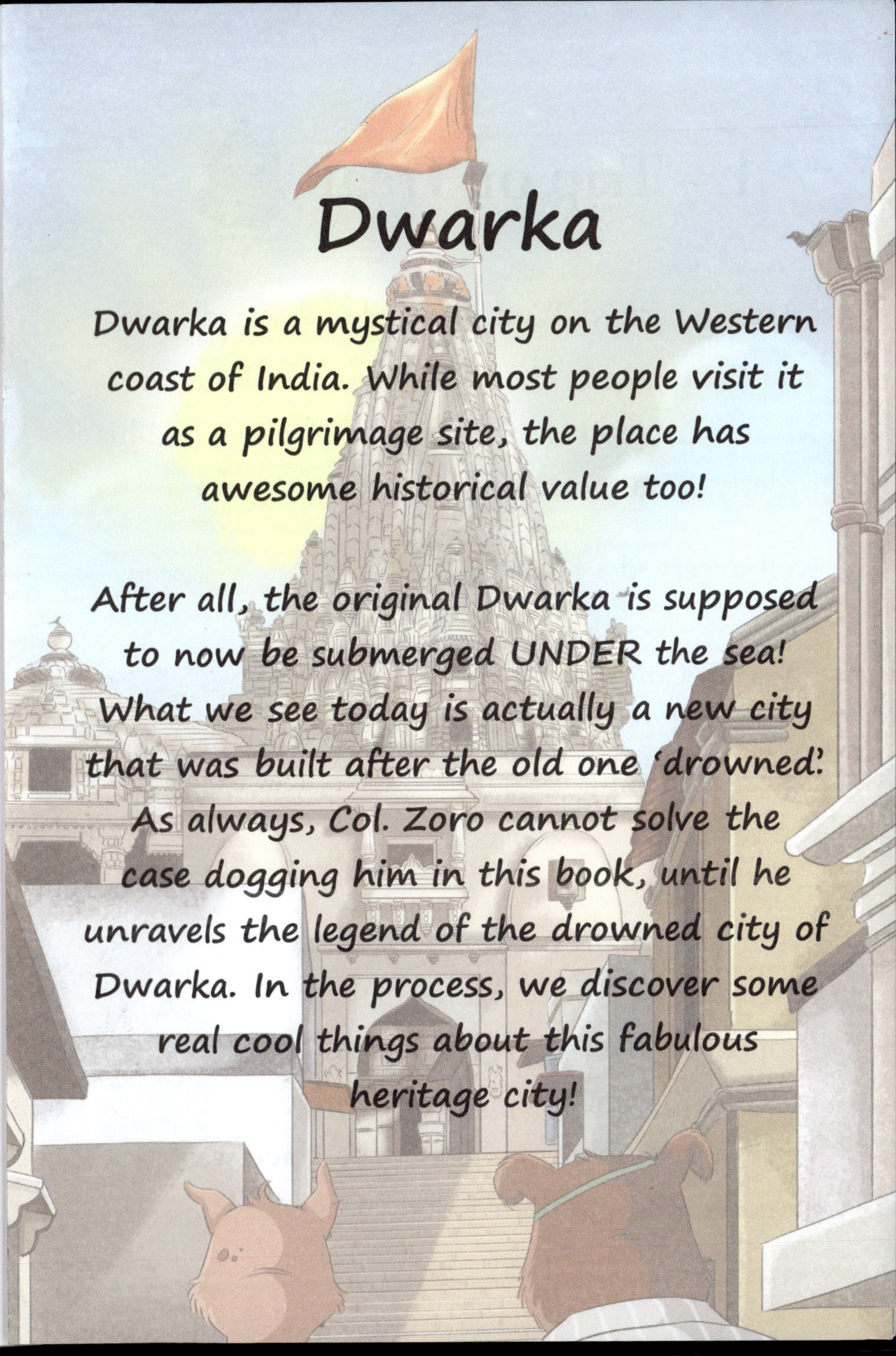

Dwarka

Dwarka is a mystical city on the Western coast of India. While most people visit it as a pilgrimage site, the place has awesome historical value too!

After all, the original Dwarka is supposed to now be submerged UNDER the sea! What we see today is actually a new city that was built after the old one 'drowned'. As always, Col. Zoro cannot solve the case dogging him in this book, until he unravels the legend of the drowned city of Dwarka. In the process, we discover some real cool things about this fabulous heritage city!

1 – Trip or Treat

“Are we packed, Wodi?” asked Col. Zoro **impatiently**. After the excitement of solving the Mystery of the Haunted Lake, Col. Zoro and his orderly, Wodi, were headed to Dwarka for a well-deserved holiday.

“Yes sir, Colonel!” saluted Wodi as he smartly wheeled the suitcases into the veranda.

Wodi was keenly looking forward to this visit. After all, Dwarka was a historical city, supposedly over **5,000** years old. Of course, some people believed that these were only rumours and the place was actually no more than 1,000 years old.

Nevertheless, Wodi lo
He was sure Dwarka
heritage buildings and
loaded the bags into th
Soon, they reached the

“Woof! Watch where yo
old boy,” growled Col. Z
as a *pariah dog** bumpe
as he got off the taxi. The
scampered away without
BACKWARD GLANC

Wodi was busy **removing** the bags and didn’t see what had happened.

*Usually a stray dog who’s breed is not kr

“What is
strugglin

“Eh, wh
lifting hi
down at

There w
from hi
he muse

Old n
were p
unfold

They f

Trip or Treat

"Return Home. If you dare come to Dwarka, you will face the wrath of the Sultan of DREAD."

"**Ooohhh**!" howled Wodi in despair. "What do we do now, sir? Should I put the bags back in the taxi?"

"Most certainly not my boy!" exclaimed Col. Zoro, licking his chops with relish. "Something tells me this holiday is going to be very interesting indeed."

Wodi tucked his **tail** between his legs as they walked into the **station.** Their train was already waiting at the platform.

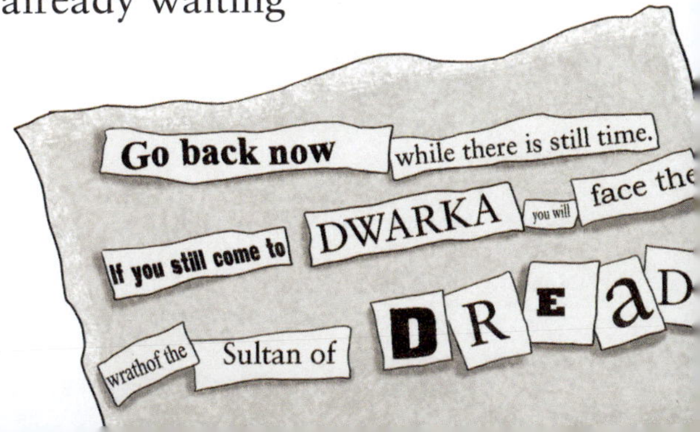

Wodi quickly stowed their baggage in the first-class compartment.

"I think a cup of Coffeecue is in order," beamed the colonel.

Wodi rushed to a stand selling piping hot **Coffeecue** and got two steaming cups, one each for Col. Zoro and himself. He knew how fond the Colonel was of this barbeque – flavoured coffee.

"Ah, **wonderful**!" said Col. Zoro, smacking his lips in satisfaction. Wodi couldn't help feeling a sense of doom, his brain swirling with thoughts of the Sultan of Dread!

FEECUE

2 – Action on Wheels

Toot, toot! The train vigorously sounded its horn and gradually pulled away from the platform. In no time, it left the station and was clicking away at good SPEED.

Col. Zoro and Wodi were comfortable, having the entire first-class coupé to themselves.

"Ah! This is wonderful," sighed Col. Zoro contentedly as he looked at the rushing scenery out of the window. "What is that you're reading, old chap?"

"It's a book called 'Adventures of Biplob the Bumblebee', sir," replied Wodi. "Quite good fun."

"Humph, aren't you a bit old to be reading this? It appears to be for CHILDREN!" remarked Col. Zoro.

"Yes sir, it is for 4-9-year-olds," replied Wodi sheepishly, "But the stories are full of adventure. It has a bee, Biplob, who is an eco-warrior. In each story, he uses an idea from nature to solve a problem. In fact..."

Before Wodi could complete his sentence, there was a knock on the door.

A uniformed Doberman came in, a tag revealing her name to be 'Laila.'

"Tickets please," asked Laila. Wodi promptly handed over their tickets to her.

Laila gasped in **SHOCK** when she saw the name on the ticket.

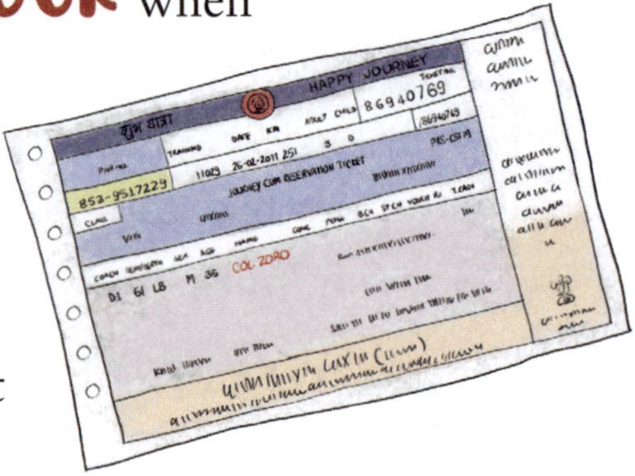

"You're the famous detective?" she asked, looking at Wodi in wonder.

"Woof, woof, that would be Col. Zorawar there," replied Wodi, pointing his snout at his boss.

Col. Zoro smiled back genially at the Doberman. His name was in all the papers after he had retrieved the *Golden Collar** from Batuk, the Bully Kutta.

**From the Detective Zoro series book 1, 'Mystery of the Haunted Lake'*

"So, you are going to Dwarka. Well, have a safe journey," said Laila **meaningfully**, before stamping their tickets and leaving.

"That was strange," said Col. Zoro, stroking his whiskers.
"Well, I'm not surprised that she recognized you," remarked Wodi. "After all, your picture was in all the papers."

"It's not that. She said '***Have a safe journey***'. Isn't that a weird thing for a ticket checker to say to the passengers? I wonder what she meant."

Little did Col. Zoro know that he would find out soon enough!

"Mmmm, this chicken broth is delicious," said Wodi, wagging his tail happily. They had just been served dinner by the pantry car.

"You like it, eh? Here, have my bowl too," offered Col. Zoro.

"Oh, I couldn't do that sir!" replied Wodi, EMBARRASSED.

"Of course you can. I'm just going to gnaw on this bone with some cottage cheese," said Col. Zoro. Wodi gladly took the additional broth while Col. Zoro contentedly gnawed on his bone.

Soon, dinner was done and they were curled up in bed.

3 – An Eventful Night

"Well, let's catch some sleep; the train reaches Dwarka at 0500 hours sharp," said Col. Zoro.

In response, there was only a snore from Wodi.

He was already *fast asleep* !

The Colonel had just shut his eyes when he sensed that someone was outside the door .

The train was now moving very **fast** and making quite a racket. However, his sixth sense had been sharpened on innumerable battlefields. Even though he couldn't hear anything, Col. Zoro was certain that there was someone outside their door.

'Never mind. I will know when they try to enter,' he thought, leaning back in his seat and **staring** at the door handle.

Sure enough, in barely a minute, someone slowly turned the handle from outside.

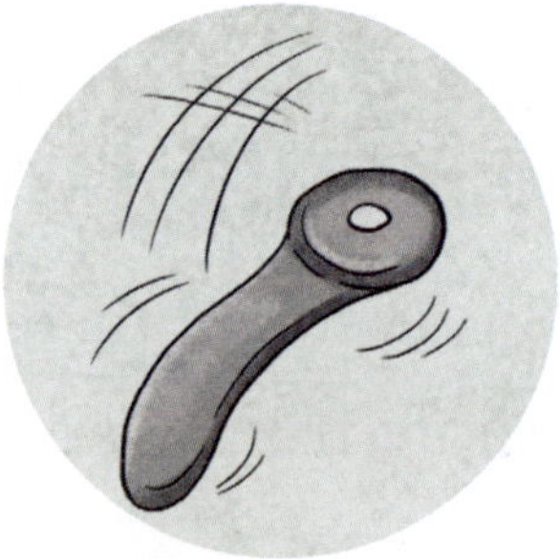

Like all good dogs, Col. Zoro could see quite well in the dark. And he wasn't any ordinary dog – he was an Indian Panther Hound!

He peered at the door through half-open eyes as a crack of light appeared and a dog silently **CREPT** in.

It was Laila, the ticket checker!

Col. Zoro didn't move, waiting to see what she wanted with them at this late hour.

Laila held a stout baton in her **PAW**. She halted between the two bunks on which Wodi and Col. Zoro slept and paused, uncertain. Then making up her mind, she turned towards the **snoring** orderly and raised her arm high, ready to strike him with the baton.

"*I wouldn't do that if I were you*," said Col. Zoro calmly, sitting up and turning on the cabin lights *simultaneously**.

**To do two or more things together, at the same time*

Laila gave a little yelp and jumped back, startled. She quickly regained her composure and instead made to **STRIKE** Col. Zoro.

However, the wily old Colonel was a veteran of many fights. He snarled at her and before she could hit him, slammed her arm with the butt of his revolver. Laila let out a proper howl this time, **FALLING** down in pain.

The baton clattered noisily to the floor. Surprisingly, Wodi slept through the entire commotion.

“Well, if it isn’t Laila the ticket checker,” remarked Col. Zoro.

As he bent down to retrieve the baton, Laila just clenched her paw, whimpering silently. "Now do you mind telling me why Wodi here is still asleep despite all the noise you've been making?" asked Col. Zoro.

Laila merely bared her **FANGS** at him in silence. "Ah, so that's how you want to play this? Very well, in that case I'll tell you what's happened," said Col. Zoro, matter-of-factly. "When you came in earlier, you were **surprised** to see us on the train."

"You have the chart with all the passenger names.

Then why were you **shocked** to see us?"

Laila maintained a stony silence, so Col. Zoro continued. "You were surprised because despite your warning, we were still on the train.

Wasn't it you who got the **pariah dog** to put this chit in my pocket?" He asked, showing the slip of paper with the warning to stay away from Dwarka.

"How did you know it was me?" asked Laila, her eyes widening in **SHOCK**.

"Simple logic my dear," informed Col. Zoro. "You were surprised that we'd got on the train despite your warning. So, you spiked our broth with something, intending to come and injure us while we were passed out.

Unfortunately for you, poor Wodi had my share of the broth too and here we are." He finished with a flourish.

"Now, the only question is, why are you hell-bent on ensuring that we don't reach Dwarka?"

"I have no choice," Laila whispered.

"They will KILL my babies otherwise."

"Babies?" Col. Zoro sniffed enquiringly.

"Yes, my four little pups.

THE SULTAN OF DREAD told me if you reach Dwarka and interfere in his plans, or if I went to the police then he would kill my babies!" sobbed Laila. "I had no choice!"

Col. Zoro looked at the **distraught** mother clutching her broken paw and instinctively knew that she was speaking the **truth**.

"Who is this Sultan of Dread?" he asked, "And why is he so **keen** on me not going to Dwarka?"

4 – The Plot Thickens

“I don’t know,” replied Laila evasively.

“I see. And was the warning that you sent us your own idea or the Sultan’s?”

“You mean that slip of paper? That was my idea.”

“Who else is helping you?” asked Col. Zoro shrewdly.

“How do you know if anyone else is helping me?” asked Laila, increasingly surprised.

“Answer me first. Who else is helping you? Are they on the train? What was the actual plan?” asked Col. Zoro sternly.

“I don’t know what you mean,” whined Laila.

"You couldn't have harmed us with this baton. Plus, YOU tried to scare us from boarding the train. Evidently, this Sultan wants you to **HARM** us but you aren't too keen on it.

Since you alone aren't **strong** enough to overpower us, I'm sure more dogs from his gang are on the train," explained Col. Zoro.

Laila sighed in resignation. "It's the chef. He spiked your broth to knock you out," she answered, "Once you were ***unconscious***, I was to help him throw you off the train...**WHAT'S THE TIME**?"

"It's 2345 hours," replied Col. Zoro.

"His plan was to come and get you at 1215AM. He should be here soon," shivered Laila, frightened.

"So, you didn't want to be responsible for our deaths and tried to **warn** us off the train. But what would you have done with this small baton of yours?" asked Col. Zoro, puzzled.

"Oh, I don't know. Maybe knock you out cold and then the cook too when he came in," sobbed Laila. "I only knew I couldn't throw you off the **RUNNING TRAIN**."

"There now, calm down," Col. Zoro reassured her. "Don't worry, everything will be fine."

"How will it be fine?" she whimpered softly, "He will surely kill my pups. **OH, MY POOR BABIES**!"

"I'll ensure nothing happens to your pups. Just do exactly as I say. Pay attention now," said Col. Zoro as he **whispered** something in Laila's ears.

She nodded quietly and left the cabin. The *intrepid** detective went back to his bunk and lay down, **pretending** to sleep.

**Someone who is extremely brave and adventurous.*

5 – A Double Agent 

At 1215AM on the dot, Col. Zoro once again saw the doorknob turn.
A swarthy bulldog in a chef cap pushed the door open and **entered**.

Laila followed, clutching the baton in her left paw.
Her right paw was in the jacket's pocket. It was Col. Zoro's idea, as that way she could rest the right paw and the cook wouldn't suspect that she was **injured**.

"Who's there?" asked Col. Zoro sleepily.
"We's come for youse, yer meddlin' mutt,"

growled the chef in a guttural drawl, advancing menacingly.

"Come for me? Are we going somewhere, my good dog?" yawned Col. Zoro, his body covered with a blanket.

"Put yer paws where I kin see 'em youse mongrel," replied the bulldog, bending over the colonel. Col. Zoro whipped off his blanket and soundly WHACKED him on the snout with his pistol.

"OW! That hurt!" squealed the bulldog.

"Not at all, old chap, but this will!" said Col. Zoro, now walloping him on the side of the head. The big bulldog collapsed in a heap.

"Well, that should put him to sleep for a few hours," beamed the colonel at Laila. "That went fine Colonel. But what now? If we reach Dwarka with you still on the train, what'll happen to my poor babies?" she **whimpered**.

"Have no fear my dear. You have the ropes I asked for?"

Laila handed him the coiled rope. Col. Zoro smiled. "Wonderful! Now, let's truss up this beast and relax till we get to Dwarka.

Once we reach, I want…" he once again **whispered** in her ear.

"What? That sounds very **dangerous**," gasped Laila.

"Not at all old girl. Don't you worry, we'll soon take care of this riffraff," beamed Col. Zoro, whiskers twitching in anticipation of the **action** to follow.

"So far, you've been an agent of this Sultan of bread or thread or whatever his name is. From now on, he will think that you're working for him but you will actually be working for me.

You are what we in Military Intelligence call **A DOUBLE AGENT**!"

6 – Gateway to Heaven

At 0500HRS, the train slowly chugged in to Dwarka station. However, Wodi showed no signs of waking up. Thankfully, neither did the chef .

“What now? Your assistant refuses to WAKE UP,” said Laila anxiously.

“Don’t worry about him. You carry on and remember my instructions,” replied Col. Zoro. Laila nodded and quickly made her way out.

As soon as she left, the Colonel called in the railway police and gave them a brief on what had transpired at night, though completely leaving out Laila’s role.

"This bulldog had an accomplice with him but I couldn't see who it was in the dark. He got away before we could catch him," explained Col. Zoro.

By now the bulldog had regained consciousness. His head was throbbing as he took in his surroundings. When his eyes fell on Col. Zoro, he scowled with intense HATRED in his eyes.

"Ha! Got you finally!" said the railway police inspector, recognizing the bulldog, "You didn't think you could get away from us forever, did you Pilloo?"

Pilloo **growled** back but that was all he could do. Col. Zoro had tied him up so well that each time he **STRUGGLED**, the knots only grew tighter!

"You know that scoundrel?" asked Col. Zoro once Pilloo was **taken away** by the constables.

They were seated in the inspector's Office, sipping on much-needed **coffeecue** waiting for Wodi to awaken.

"Yes, Pilloo is an old criminal and we have been after him for many **YEARS** now," replied the inspector, whose name was Chloe.

"We suspect he's involved in the smuggling racket in Dwarka," she added

"Smuggling racket? What could these criminals be smuggling into Dwarka?" asked Col. Zoro between sips of his coffeecue.

"Not smuggling into, Colonel," replied Chloe grimly, "But out of Dwarka. And let me tell you, it is probably the most valuable thing any nation can have!"

"Interesting. And what does Dwarka have that is so valuable?"

"Don't you know? Why, it is our heritage!" replied Chloe indignantly.

Gateway to Heaven

"I know Dwarka is a very old and **HISTORIC** city, but how can someone 'smuggle' its heritage?" asked Col. Zoro, puzzled.

"A pack of dogs is smuggling old idols and *artefacts* from Dwarka, Colonel. Some of these could be as old as 7000 BCE," the inspector revealed.

Col. Zoro was shocked. That was *unbelievable*! No existing **civilization** was that old. How then could there be artefacts in Dwarka that were from 7000 BCE?

"You know what the name 'Dwarka' means?" asked Chloe, continuing.

"Dwarka means 'Doorway to Heaven'. You should meet Professor Victorious. He'll be able to guide you and who knows, you might help us break up this pack of smugglers," explained Chloe.

Before he could reply, Wodi woke up **groaning**. "Are you fine, old dog?" asked Col. Zoro, concerned.

"Yes, seems like I *overslept*," replied a confused Wodi.

The Colonel howled in delight. "Not exactly but don't worry. I'll explain everything **ON THE WAY**. Come along then and say toodle-oo to inspector Chloe here."

7 – A Mysterious Tail

They took a taxi to their hotel, the Ritz Canine. As the car snaked through the bustling streets of Dwarka, Col. Zoro filled Wodi in on all that he'd missed.

"So where is Laila now?" asked Wodi.

"Escaped, unfortunately. I suppose she's returned to her masters to report on what's happened," explained Col. Zoro as they reached the hotel.

They quickly checked in and collected their keys. As they walked towards the elevators to get to their room, Col. Zoro noticed the receptionist was surreptitiously TELEPHONING someone.

'So now the villains know we've **arrived**... this is getting more and more intriguing,' he thought to himself.

After a quick breakfast, they took a **TAXI** to get to Professor Victorious' office.

Chloe had said that he headed the Department of Archaeological Survey.
"What's an archaeological survey?" asked Wodi.

Col. Zoro explained, "It's an office where **ARCHAEOLOGISTS** work."
Wodi looked even more puzzled.

"An archaeologist is someone who studies *history* through old buildings and *artefacts*," the Colonel added patiently.

"Archaeologists dig up **OLD CITIES** and can even find out how old something is.

Many years back, British archaeologists found out that Dwarka is nearly 1,000 years old," explained Col. Zoro.

Wodi seemed distracted though. "Sir, I think we are being **followed**," he said.

"And when did you make that discovery, my good dog?" asked Col. Zoro generously. "I just saw two dogs on a motorcycle. They were at the previous **turning** too and unless they're also going to meet the archaeologists, I'm sure they're following us."

TAXI

A Mysterious Tail

"Well done indeed, Wodi!"
Col. Zoro grinned.

"They are actually following us since we left the hotel. I'm impressed you noticed them eventually. I guess we will make a detective out of you yet."

Wodi LOOKED *bemused**. His boss was actually happy at being followed by dangerous dogs!

They'd stopped at a traffic light, with the dogs right behind them.

"When the light turns green, move the taxi to the left and stop," Col. Zoro instructed the driver, who wagged his tail in response.

**Puzzled, confused or completely bewildered.*

Once the light turned green, their taxi pulled over, allowing other vehicles to pass. The dogs following them also stopped, *puzzled*. Suddenly, Col. Zoro yelled, "Quick! Turn left," the driver instantly swerved left with a loud screech. Before the other dogs could react, the light turned **red** again. They were stranded at the signal!

"There. We've lost our **tail**," beamed Col. Zoro.
"Wha...?" said Wodi, shocked. He looked back but his tail was still there. "I don't know about you sir, but thankfully my tail is still here!"

"Not that, Wodi. In detective parlance 'tail' is a code – word for someone **FOLLOWING** you," explained Col. Zoro .

"Oh, right," said Wodi, **embarrassed**.

When they reached his office, they found that Professor Victorious was a conscientious *Labrador Retriever** .

"I should have known that the head of the archaeology department will be a retriever. After all, what is archelogy but 'retrieving' very old stuff!" whispered Col. Zoro as they **WAITED** to see the professor.

**A dog – breed known for its ability to 'retrieve' stuff from far away! Earlier used by hunters to fetch their kill, they are now everyone's favourite companions.*

Suddenly, they heard a low **growl** from inside the cabin. Though they couldn't make out what was being said, it was **clear** that it was nothing good.

"Quick, get here," said Col. Zoro as he jumped behind the sofa, pulling Wodi with him.

They were in the **NICK OF TIME**.

Just then, the door opened and out walked a huge Bully Kutta, followed by three mean-looking pariah dogs!

Once the dogs **left**, they got up and went into the professor's cabin.

8 – Finding the Victorious

"How may I help Colonel?" said Professor Victorious nervously, "Fancy the army coming to **meet** me!"

"I'm only a retired Colonel, professor, now working as a private detective," replied Col. Zoro. "I was actually wondering if I could be of **assistance** to you."

"Why would I need the help of a private detective?" asked the professor innocently.

"Why indeed, professor, why indeed. That's the big **QUESTION**, isn't it?" asked Col. Zoro, his eye gleaming.

"Huh? I'm sure I don't know what you mean," stammered the Labrador Retriever.

“Don’t you? You head the archaeology department. If a pack of dogs is smuggling artefacts from Dwarka, either you are aware of it, or worse, you are a part of the plot to steal our heritage,” announced Col. Zoro dramatically. Even Wodi was startled!

“Wh...wh...what smugglers?” stammered Victorious. “I...I...I don’t know anything. PUH...PUH...please leave, I am very busy.”

“Come now, professor. Surely you don’t expect me to believe that those hooligans that just left were here on a SOCIAL VISIT?” asked Col. Zoro casually.

“Wasn’t that the Sultan of Dread that just left after THREATENING you?”

The professor visually crumbled hearing this. “Yes, it was,” he admitted. “He threatened that if I even breathed a word to anyone, he would kill me. I don’t want to help him but I don’t know what to do.”

“Do not fret, professor,” reassured Col. Zoro.

“We are here now. In fact, whatever he told you, I’m sure it has to do with us being here. He’s already tried killing us once and failed.”

ARCTIC OCEAN
PACIFIC OCEAN

"We will get him before he does any more harm. Now, tell me **everything**." Instructed Col. Zoro.

"What do you wish to know?" asked the professor, regaining some of his **composure**.

"Well, we know that you have made some important discoveries in Dwarka..."

"How do you know that? We haven't told anyone yet!" **interrupted** the professor in surprise.

"Logical old dog! After being a forgotten town for so long, suddenly there is a pack of international smugglers operating in Dwarka."

Finding the Victorious

"Then, there is the world – famous archaeologist Professor Victorious working here. What does that tell you? Simple, that the professor, that is you, has made some IMPORTANT discoveries.

The smugglers are here to either steal whatever it is that you have found, or keep the knowledge of your finds from the rest of the world!"

announced Col. Zoro grandly.

"You are right, Colonel," nodded Professor Victorious, impressed.

"Let me tell you a story."

"How old do you think Dwarka is?" asked Professor Victorious, getting into teacher mode.

"Umm, I think it was formed around **500CE**?" guessed Wodi.

"Yes, that is what British historians would have us believe. I don't blame them, for the information available at that time indicated that that is how old Dwarka is.

But, our research now shows us the place is older. **Much, much older**. Do you know about the Mahabharat?" said Professor Victorious.

"Yes, of course!" replied Col. Zoro.

9 – A Victorious ‘Tail’ 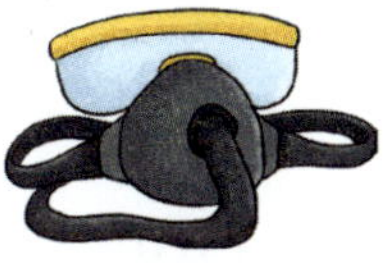

“It is the epic mythological tale of a great war between the Pandavs and Kauravs, two sets of cousins,” he answered.

“What if the Mahabharat isn’t just mythology?” whispered Professor Victorious.

“What do you mean?”

“The Mahabharat states that Lord Krishna, who was charioteer to the great Pandav warrior, Arjun, was the king of Dwarka. Now, various INSCRIPTIONS and findings tell us that the Mahabharat war actually happened around 3100BCE. This means, that Dwarka is at least in existence since 3100 BCE,” explained the professor.

"Hmmm, that is interesting. I remember reading about a study carried out by the **world-famous** physicist *DR. Narahari Achar**," recalled Col. Zoro. "Using astronomy, he also proved that the Mahabharat war took place around 3000 BCE."

"Er… sorry, but what is **astronomy**?" asked Wodi meekly.

"Astronomy, my good dog, is the study of planets, stars and suns. Professor Achar was an **EXPERT** in Archaeoastronomy – the study of astronomy and archaeology," beamed Col. Zoro.

**Dr Narhari Achar, professor of physics at the University of Memphis, was a pioneering archaeoastronomer who dated the Mahabharata war to 3067BCE and Krishna's birth at 3112BC.*

"Oooh, my head is spinning," moaned Wodi. "Please can we just talk about catching smugglers and gangsters?"

"Anyway, you are right detective," laughed the professor. "We did some digging on our own to get to the truth. If DR. Achar's astronomical data is correct, then the original city of Dwarka – Krishna's Dwarka – is now under the sea."

"UNDER THE SEA?" asked Wodi, looking scared.

"Yes, legends say that the old Dwarka got submerged under the sea. So, if it did exist, it would now be underwater," explained Prof. Victorious.

A Victorious 'Tail'

"For the last six months, our divers have been exploring the coast off present – day Dwarka and have retrieved **priceless** *relics** from the original Dwarka of Lord Krishna!"

"And? Do these prove that Dwarka is at least from 3000BCE?" asked Col. Zoro, leaning forward in excitement.

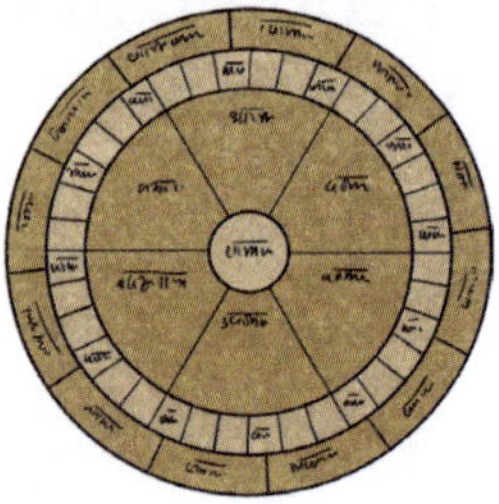

"No...they prove that Dwarka dates back to at least 7500 BCE!" exclaimed the professor.

Everyone gaped in shock. Even Col. Zoro was rendered momentarily speechless.

"**WHAT**!" he managed to find his voice again.

** These are objects or articles from the distant past, like idols, artefacts and carvings*

"This changes the entire course of **history**," said Wodi. "Everything we know will have to be revised, if an advanced civilization existed as far back as *7500 BCE**!"

"Your research may also **PROVE** that the Mahabharat isn't just mythology!" added Col. Zoro, "But something that actually happened."

"Indeed," agreed the professor. "And **imagine** the value of the artefacts we've retrieved from under the sea. They could be the oldest antiques in the world, making them **invaluable** to a collector."

** Underwater archaeologists from the Indian National Institute of Ocean Technology Carbon dated one of the wooden samples from the Gulf of Cambay, where Dwarka is submerged. It was found to be from around 7500 BC.*

"I have a question, professor," said Col. Zoro thoughtfully, "How are you so sure that the artefacts you **found** are actually this old?"

"Good question," nodded Victorious, "With a simple answer. **carbon dating**!"

"What now? Another new – fangled word!" moaned Wodi.

"Carbon dating is a method of calculating the age of something. You simply measure the amounts of different forms of carbon in them. It is actually very **ACCURATE**!" explained Vicotrious.

"When we carbon dated the artefacts retrieved from Dwarka, they were found to be from around 7500BCE. Now imagine if those antiques are lost FOREVER because someone steals them?" asked the professor seriously.

"What do you mean? Wait, are you saying that if those artefacts are stolen, then you cannot prove for sure that Dwarka dates back to nearly 7500BCE?" said Col. Zoro, *incredulous**.

"Exactly! Those artefacts are the only proof that the Mahabharat and ancient Dwarka are not a myth but real, legitimate history."

* *Shocked and surprised at hearing something that is unbelievable.*

10 – Missing Pieces of History

Col. Zoro and Wodi were STUNNED by what they'd just heard.

"One thing is clear – this Sultan of Dread is no ordinary smuggler," said Col. Zoro finally. "He is surely working for some very POWERFUL dogs. What did he want from you?"

"Small artefacts and other material have been going MISSING from our finds over the last few months," announced Victorious miserably.

"At first I thought maybe the material was simply misplaced. However, I realized that wasn't the case when we started missing some rather important pieces."

"How did you **discover** that things were missing?" asked Col. Zoro.

"Once in **15** days, all the artefacts are sent to the capital city in a special compartment on the train. I load the artefacts here and lock the compartment. Once the train *reaches* the city, my boss there uses his key to open the compartment and **remove** everything.

Initially, the Archaeology office in the capital wrote to us saying that a few pieces were **missing**.

Gradually, the number and importance of missing pieces kept **increasing**."

"And there are only two **keys** to open this compartment – one with you and the other with your boss?" asked Col. Zoro.

The professor nodded in confirmation. Then suddenly said, "Say, do you know swimming? Yes? Splendid, let me show you what this Sultan of Dread wants from me."

He got up from his seat and headed out of his cabin, Col. Zoro and Wodi in tow. "Where are we going?" asked Col. Zoro as they sat in the professor's car, winding through the STREETS of Dwarka.

"There!" Professor Victorious **pointed** to a shining boat bobbing on the waves.

Soon, they **boarded** the salvage ship and sailed out a few miles into the water.

"This is the SS Balti," explained Victorious. "We use her to go on our dives . Put on these scuba suits and I will show you what that dreaded Sultan of Thread is after." "Er... no. Thank you but I'll pass," said Wodi, shrinking away from the scuba gear that the professor was **OFFERING** him. "What's the matter?" asked the professor.

"Wodi is a dog that hates getting wet," explained Col. Zoro, putting on his suit. Then turning to Wodi, he winked, "Better put it on, old dog. You'll find it decidedly easy to breathe with one of these."

"You mean..." sputtered Wodi.

"Exactly. Put it on or in 3 minutes I'm pushing you in the water, scuba suit or not," barked Col. Zoro.

He knew Wodi would walk off a cliff or into a hail of bullets for him but even wild Rottweilers couldn't DRAG him into water!

Short of threatening to throw him in, Col. Zoro knew nothing would work. With a hangdog expression, Wodi put on the suit. "Isn't that better now?" beamed Col. Zoro.

Once they were suited up and had run through all the checks, they dived in with a splash. The professor **guided** them deep into the sea, the darkness growing thicker with each foot that they descended. Luckily, a small lamp attached to each of their helmets illuminated the path ahead, allowing them to see clearly under water.

In a few minutes, they were staring at the **RUINS** of what was undoubtedly an ancient city!

The professor gestured and they headed down into the ruins. As they swam closer, Col. Zoro saw remnants of old houses, palaces and roads. It was **unbelievable** that such a huge city existed so close to the modern Dwarka.

Then suddenly, as if like **magic**, they came upon a massive building – or what would have been a massive building, from the size of the broken stone walls.

They **followed** the professor through a maze of the walls and found huge, intricately carved stone pillars.

There were four pillars, each nearly 10 feet in diameter and still standing 30 feet **tall**! They had beautiful carvings of trees, animals, plants, planets, battle scenes, angels, kings and queens.

The three simply waded there, admiring the magnificent, mesmerising **STRUCTURES**.

Eventually it was time and the professor **signalled** for them to return to the SS Balti.

"Those pillars are **splendid** professor," marvelled Col. Zoro once they were back on the boat, sipping warm cups of Coffeecue.

"Once you retrieve them, they will without a doubt **prove** the existence of the old city of Dwarka."

"Exactly, Colonel. Carbon dating the pillars will prove how old the city is. And imagine if just the pillars are so **MASSIVE**, how huge the palace must have been.

This means the people from 7500BCE were **advanced** enough to know how to make such big buildings!"

11 – Sultan of Dread

"You'd asked what that Sultan of Dread wants from me – he has DECIDED to steal the entire compartment which will be carrying the pillars to the city," said Professor Victorious.

Wodi SPUTTERED into his cup. "How does one steal a whole train compartment?"

"I don't know," answered the professor, worried sick. "All I know is that he threatened to kill me and all my staff if the pillars aren't loaded onto the train compartment by **tomorrow night**."

"Have no fear professor; we shall be **VICTORIOUS**," joked Col. Zoro. "You load the pillars onto the train.

LEAVE THE REST TO ME.

Just remember one thing though, don't breathe a word to anyone that you told us about these pillars and what this Sultan of thread PLANS to do."

By now they'd reached the shore. Col. Zoro once again **reminded** Professor Victorious to keep their meeting a secret before getting into a taxi to return to the hotel.

"Onwards to the Dwarkadhish temple my dog," said Col. Zoro cheerily to the taxi driver.

"I thought we were **RETURNING** to the hotel?" exclaimed Wodi. After the trauma of diving in the ocean, the last thing he wanted was another adventure!

"We will, Wodi but first, we meet our **secret agent**," said Col. Zoro enigmatically.

"After all, there is a very **interesting** mystery to solve.
Consider this: A compartment has only two keys, one is in Dwarka with Professor Victorious."

"The other key is with his boss in the head office. Before the compartment leaves Dwarka, the professor **LOCKS** it.

However, when the compartment reaches the city and the Top Dog opens it, there are things missing from it. How is that *possible*?"

"I don't know. My head hurts with all these complicated questions," moaned Wodi.

"That is exactly what we have to find out.

Who will go to all this **trouble** to harm us?"

"Do you see what is at stake here – it is the very **PRIDE** of our country."

Wodi suddenly perked up. "I know! The **Chinese Chowchows**! I'm sure they are behind all this. They always have a bone to pick with us," he growled menacingly.

"Agreed. I'm pretty sure they're acting through their loyal allies, the Bully Kuttas. Now let's see what our agent has to say," nodded Col. Zoro as the **MAGNIFICENT** Dwarkadhish Temple came into view.

12 – Double Trouble

They stood a little away from The Dwarkadhish temple that towered high above the surrounding houses and shops. The highest tower had a massive flag fluttering in the breeze and they could see the steps of the temple leading to the river which flowed gently alongside.

"Did you know, sir, this temple was first CONSTRUCTED around 500BCE," stated Wodi as they stood gazing at the massive, intricately carved temple structure.

"Really?" asked Col. Zoro, glancing at Wodi. "Yes. Through the centuries several invaders have destroyed the temple," added Wodi.

"Only for it to be reconstructed,
more **magnificent** than before!"
he reverentially looked at the temple.

"Quick, in here before we are seen," whispered a **hoarse** voice. Col. Zoro and Wodi turned and followed the voice through a dark doorway. Being dogs, dark places held no fear for them.

"Did you get my message across, Laila?" asked Col. Zoro once they were in the dark room.

"Yes, detective, I did. Now you only need to tell me the time and **LOCATION** so I can pass it on."

"Laila? The ticket checker?" asked Wodi, BEWILDERED.

"Yes, Wodi. Laila is a double agent. The villains think she is working for them whereas she is actually working for us," announced Col. Zoro.

While he had told Wodi about the attack the previous night, he had left out the part about recruiting Laila.

"What time? Which location? What is she talking about?" asked Wodi, thoroughly confused now.

"All will be revealed in good time, my dog, all in good time," replied Col. Zoro.

Turning to Laila, Col. Zoro went on, "There is a very important CONSIGNMENT on the train tomorrow night. Apparently, this Sultan is planning to steal the entire compartment. Has he told you how he PLANS to do that?"

"Not yet," Laila replied, "but I'm meeting him later tonight. Probably that is when he will tell me."

She paused and her tail flagged suddenly. "What about my poor pups? I haven't seen them in several weeks and I am now very WORRIED," she whimpered softly.

"Ah yes, the pups," said Col. Zoro, "Sultan of bread will have to stop the train to de-link one compartment.

He will need you for that. I **SUSPECT** this is his last act before he leaves Dwarka for good.

Once he pulls off this **robbery**, his work is done.

So, you listen to his plan and **agree** to do everything he asks of you but on one condition – he has to bring your pups with him when he comes to rob the train."

“Oh, he won’t agree,” **howled** Laila with grief.

“He certainly will,” countered Col. Zoro. “Once this job is done, he has no further use for you and has nothing to **lose** by bringing the pups there.

On the contrary, he can use them to **ensure** you do exactly as he says!”

Laila stopped howling and nodded.

What Col. Zoro said made perfect sense. She calmed down and left, **promising** to return later that night to debrief him after meeting the enemy.

"How about a spot of lassi before we trot along eh, old dog?" suggested Col. Zoro to Wodi.

"Lord Krishna was terribly fond of butter and buttermilk. I'm sure they still have the best buttermilk ever in Dwarka."

They stepped out of the dark hut and walked along to one of the shops. Soon, they were ambling back to their hotel, SIPPING on delicious buttermilk from small earthen pots, licking their chops and wagging their tails happily.

13 – Wodi in Trouble

"Mmmm...this is really good," mumbled Wodi, his mouth full of lassi.

"Quite right," replied Col. Zoro, taking a long satisfying slurp. "You see, Lord Krishna grew up among cow herders and obviously, they have the best milk and make the best milk products."

They were so involved in savouring their treat, they didn't realise that they'd wandered into a deserted lane. Three menacing looking pariah dogs stood before them!

Wodi slowed down as he took in his surroundings. "This does not look good, sir," he gulped, looking at the three menacing pariah dogs standing before them.

"It's not as bad as it seems....until you look behind of course," replied Col. Zoro, nonchalantly **SIPPING** on his lassi.

"Behind?" Wodi turned around. **BLOCKING** off their exit stood three more pariahs with bared fangs! Wodi let out a low moan, "Oh no, this doesn't look good at all."

"I think you're right," replied Col. Zoro, **staring** into his glass. "This doesn't look good at all. I'm all out of lassi – and just when I was really beginning to **ENJOY** it!"

"That's the only good thing, sir," answered Wodi, taking up a **defensive** taekwondo stance. "At least now your paws will be free to fight." Col. Zoro merely snorted in response.

The dogs in front began advancing slowly towards them, FANGS BARED.

"Excellent teeth, fellows," remarked Col. Zoro genially. "Could you refer me to your dentist? I'd like to CONGRATULATE her myself!"

"Think youse is very funny, eh? Wees is gonna repair your tiths ourselves with these!" said the leader in broken English, pointing to the stout stick he held.

"I don't think so, old chap. Now if only your English teacher had been as efficient as your dentist, you'd not be speaking like this," replied Col. Zoro, flinging his empty glass at the dog's head.

"OW!" yelped the leader of the pariahs as the earthen container hit him square on the snout.

He DROPPED his stick and ran away, clutching his bleeding snout.

"Good aim, sir!" said Wodi, admiringly. By then, the dogs from behind had reached them.

Wodi in Trouble

Wodi smartly kicked the pack leader on his paw. The pariah dropped his stick and clutched his paw in **PAIN**.

"Yes, well, you know I've always been a good *fielder* in cricket," said Col. Zoro humbly, taking Wodi's glass of lassi from his paws.

He **flung** the container at the other two dogs. It hit one of them on the head with a resounding sound, while the salted buttermilk still remaining in the glass splashed into the eyes of the other dog.

The blinded dog howled in pain and **BUMPED** into his companion, both falling down in a heap. With loud yelps, they tucked their tails and ran for dear life.

Seeing their companions **DESERT** them, the other two pariahs decided they'd had enough.

Snarling at Col. Zoro, they slinked away into a side lane.

"*That wasn't bad*," said Wodi, dusting himself.

"Yes, I told you the lassi here is **outstanding**," replied Col. Zoro as they made their way to the hotel. "I didn't know the containers too are so good!"

14 – Teas and Cakes 

"Ah, I think I'll have a nice cheese sandwich with some Coffeecue," said Col. Zoro, sprawling on the **comfortable** sofa in their hotel room. "Would you like something, Wodi?"

"The same, sir, if you don't mind," said Wodi, as he sat down next to the colonel.

Col. Zoro **ORDERED** for the food on room service.

They'd both been reviewing the facts of the case when a few minutes later, there was a knock on the door.

"**ROOM SERVICE**!"

Wodi open the door to a dog who looked like anything but a waiter. He was a **WELL-BUILT** Rottweiler whose muscles bulged through his uniform. He carried himself erect like a soldier.

The Rottweiler nodded to Wodi and made his way inside the room, **BEARING** a tray with their sandwiches.

"There you are and about time," beamed Col. Zoro. The waiter placed the tray on the coffee table and handed Col. Zoro the bill.

"Alright, Wodi, ***let's be off***," said the detective once the waiter left.

09

"Be off? I thought we were going to eat," said a **puzzled** Wodi.

"Of course we are…as soon as we return from our rendezvous," replied Col. Zoro, removing the bill from his pocket. "This is a note from Laila asking to **meet** us at a café around the corner. Let's see what she has to share."

The café was **crowded** with dogs of all kinds and breeds, having Coffeecue, pastries, scones and other delicious fare.

"There, through that door," *whispered* the dog in-charge.

Col. Zoro and Wodi made their way quietly through the door the dog in-charge was pointing at and entered a small, dimly lit room.

"What have you got for us, Laila? I hope it is better than these cakes and pastries here," asked Col. Zoro, fixing her with a **PENETRATING LOOK**.

Laila looked a little shaken up. "He wants me to stop the train in the middle of the **forest**, where he plans to do something with the archaeologist's compartment."

"Once the train stops, I'm supposed to get off and head into the **WOODS**."

"What about your pups?" enquired Col. Zoro.

"He said as soon as the train stops, they will hand over my *babies* to me."

"I see," said Col. Zoro, thoughtfully biting into a cream scone while Wodi slurped on a Coffeecue. "There is **nothing to worry** about, Laila. Go on as planned. We will take care of the rest." Saying this, they made their way back to the Ritz Canine.

"What now sir?" asked Wodi once they returned.

"Now, we finish these poor cheese sandwiches that are waiting for us," replied Col. Zoro,

BITING into a cheesy morsel. "And tomorrow morning we pay a visit to Professor Victorious and then the railway station."

"**Railway station**? Are we leaving already? Why Professor Victorious? We just met him today!" exclaimed Wodi.

"**Patience**, my good dog. All is revealed to the patient dog, don't you know?" said Col. Zoro, as he curled up to sleep, his stomach full.

15 – Wheels in Motion

Next morning, after a hearty breakfast they headed out to complete their **ERRANDS**.

"Can you go to the booking counter and purchase tickets for us to leave after three days?" suggested Col. Zoro once they reached the railway station.

"What will we do for **three more days** here, sir?" asked Wodi.

"Rest and **relaxation** are in order my good dog," winked Col. Zoro.

Wodi went on his way to carry out the strange instructions. Meanwhile, the Colonel headed to meet Inspector Chloe.

"Can you arrange for two porter uniforms?" he asked the Inspector.

"Yes, but why?" asked a puzzled Chloe.

"I suspect Sultan of Sweat will make a move soon and I want to be here when that happens. No one will find a porter **OUT OF PLACE** at a railway station. We can quietly observe all the goings-on without attracting any unwanted attention to ourselves," explained Col. Zoro

"That's smart thinking!" remarked Chloe.

Col. Zoro left, **PROMISING** to collect the uniforms later that evening.

"Here are the tickets, Colonel," said Wodi when he returned.

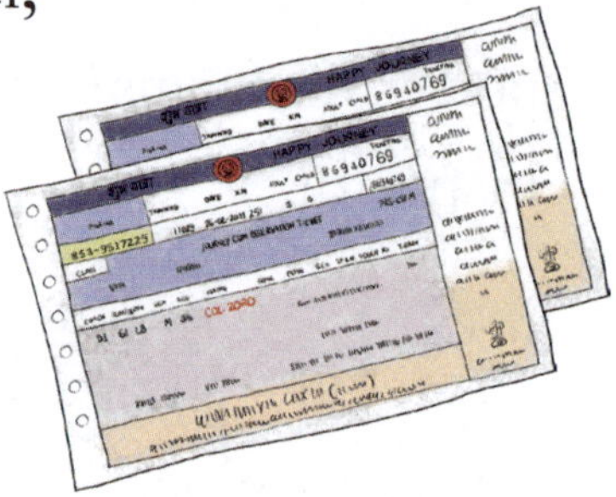

"I found the booking clerk very weird though."

"Did you now? How is that?"

"I saw her picking up the telephone and **CALLING** someone as soon as she thought my back was turned. It was as if she was informing someone about when we were leaving the city."

"**Excellent**," grinned Col. Zoro,

"Exactly as I wanted it. Come on then, let's carry on and see the good Professor."

A thoroughly CONFUSED Wodi followed Col. Zoro as they took a taxi to the professor's office.

"I hope you're all set for moving the pillars today?" asked Col. Zoro when they reached.

"Sadly, I am," replied the retriever, his ears drooping sadly. "It's a Pity about what they will do to these marvellous finds."

"Oh pish-tosh, old dog, nothing will happen to them," asserted Col. Zoro. "Now, please take me to the CARTONS in which you will put the pillars."

"Cartons? What do you want with them?" asked the professor. Without waiting for an answer though, he led them to a huge **Shed** at the back of the office building.

Inside were **four cartons**, each as big as a small house.

"These are excellent!" exclaimed Col. Zoro, sizing up the **massive boxes**.

"Wodi, why don't you escort Professor Victorious back, while I inspect the cartons and make sure everything is **secure**. The professor doesn't look too good."

“You are right, Colonel. My head is spinning thinking about the poor pillars and what that villain will do to them,” the professor said dejectedly as Wodi started to escort him back to his office.

“If only I could save them… imagine, the whole world will have proof that Dwarka is an ancient city and krishna did indeed exist!”

“Yes, quite a tragedy,” replied Col. Zoro. “Anyway, we shall do our best!”

Soon, they were done and returned to the Ritz Canine hotel.

16 – Twist in the Tail

After lunch, Col. Zoro again asked a surprised Wodi to get ready to **LEAVE**.

"Where to now, sir?" he asked.

"Now, we visit the **kitchen** of this fine establishment," replied Col. Zoro.

"Huh? Do you wish to find out how they **COOK**?"

"That would be nice but not today, old dog, not today. Today, we enter the kitchen," replied Col. Zoro, ***opening the door*** to the kitchen, "So we may exit from the back door without being detected by the Sultan's minions."

Col. Zoro grabbed two chef caps on the way out. Disguised as cooks, they quietly walked in the direction of the market.

"It seems we've MANAGED to lose them, sir," said Wodi.

"As usual you're right, my dog," said Col. Zoro, discarding his chef cap in a handy garbage bin before hailing a taxi. "To the railway station," he said to the taxi driver.

Though puzzled as to why they were returning to the railway station, Wodi remained silent.

After all, nothing they'd been doing since last evening made any **sense** to him!

At the station, things got even more confusing. Instead of the front entrance, they went to the **BACKYARD** where old **JUNK** was stored.

There, Col. Zoro retrieved two porter uniforms and put one on, *handing* the other to Wodi.

"Sir?" asked Wodi, **HOLDING HIS UNIFORM**.

"Put it on. As porters we don't need to buy tickets to get on any train.

Imagine how much fun we can have!"

'It seems the poor Colonel has had a sunstroke while diving yesterday,' thought Wodi to himself as he donned his uniform. 'Let me humour him.'

They wandered around the platform for the next couple of hours, mixing with the other dogs passing through. Finally, it was time for the train to the CAPITAL CITY.

There was a sense of expectation as the train chugged onto the platform and stopped so passengers could board.

Everyone watched AWESTRUCK as the four massive cartons were carried in on a crane and loaded into the special compartment.

The compartment itself had been modified.

It was now DOUBLE its usual size.

"In three days, we shall be on this same train," said Wodi wistfully.

"Three days? Rubbish my dog. Surely you didn't think we're wearing these porter uniforms because it's the *latest rage* in Doggie fashion?" said Col. Zoro.

"We're wearing them so we may BOARD this train without attracting attention," he said, surreptitiously getting on the train.

A dazed Wodi followed him; this day was getting stranger by the minute!

17 – Jack in the Box

As the train slowly pulled away, they made their way towards the compartment adjacent to the pillars.

"So that's your plan!" said Wodi once they were **SEATED**. "When the Sultan comes to **ROB** the train, you will stop him."

"Stop him? **ABSOLUTELY NOT**!

We are only here because these are the best seats in the house to **WATCH** the show as the Sultan of Fret attacks the train when it stops," said Col. Zoro, happily sipping on the Coffeecue he'd bought from the pantry car.

"B…But I thought we were going to **stop** him from stealing the pillars," said Wodi, trying hard to make sense of everything.

"Pillars? What pillars? Who said anything about pillars? Surely Wodi, you don't mean those pillars that could be as old as 7500BCE?" asked Col. Zoro with **mock** surprise.

"Yes exactly, isn't that what the Sultan is coming to steal?" questioned Wodi.
"Oh, right. Well, he thinks that is what he is coming to steal. Unfortunately, there are no **PILLARS** on this train."

"What! Then what's inside those huge boxes in the next compartment? And where are the **PILLARS** ?"

Before Col. Zoro could reply, the train tooted loudly and started slowing down.

"Quiet now, Wodi...the show begins!" said Col. Zoro gleefully, **POLISHING** off his Coffeecue.

Sure enough, in a couple of minutes, the train ground to a halt amidst a dense forest.

It was so dark outside that one could barely see more than a few feet away in any direction. The train looked bright and cheerful in contrast.

Soon, they could make out some lights dancing in the woods ahead.

"Come Wodi, that is our cue to disembark," said Col. Zoro. Wodi *quietly* followed as the colonel disembarked from the train.

They hid in the space between their compartment and the one that BELONGED to the archaeology department.

As the lights moved closer, they saw that it was a whole pack of pariah dogs, led by none other than the **SULTAN OF DREAD**!

"Where are my babies?" they heard Laila ask. The Bully Kutta gestured to one of the pariah dogs. He was CARRYING a basket covered with a cloth, which he handed over to Laila.

She opened the cloth to reveal four of the most adorable puppies ever! They licked their mother, happy to see her again, as she squealed with delight.

"Off with you now; let us do our job," snapped the Bully Kutta.

"And remember, if this train moves for the next 15 minutes, I'll come back and get your pups," warned the Sultan of Dread.

Wodi and Col. Zoro watched in silence as the pariahs produced a key and opened the compartment. They clambered up, their tails wagging slowly with satisfaction and opened the first of the four huge boxes inside.

Before they could react, they found automatic rifles pointed directly at them.

Instead of pillars, the boxes contained **MILITARY COMMANDOS** !

A fierce fight broke out between the two packs of dogs but the pariahs were no MATCH for the SUPREMELY well-trained Rottweilers.

In a matter of minutes, the smugglers were OVERPOWERED and trussed up by the commandos!

"Well done, Captain Tipu," congratulated Col. Zoro as he emerged from his hiding spot. "I knew I could depend on you."

"At your command, Colonel," said Captain Tipu, as he and the other Rottweilers smartly saluted their ex-commander.

"These scoundrels will be taken to PRISON to pay for their crimes."

18 – The Detective's Masterplan

"That was amazing colonel. How did you manage to **PULL** that off?" asked Laila. It was a happy pack of dogs that sat in the pantry car as the train merrily chugged on towards its **DESTINATION**.

"Nothing **AMAZING** there, Laila, if you think about it," replied Col. Zoro modestly, licking his chops.

"Once I **KNEW** what this Sultan of Thread or whatever his name is had planned, I **SWITCHED** the boxes carrying the pillars with those hiding Captain Tipu and his men."

"To deceive them, Wodi booked our train tickets for three days from now.

As I suspected, the booking officer immediately called the GANG and told them.

After that it was a simple matter of us pretending to be porters and getting onto this train," explained Col. Zoro.

"So that is why you had us leave the hotel disguised as cooks," exclaimed Wodi, "and here I thought that you were not well and hence were behaving so strangely!"

"Ha ha, not at all Wodi, I've never been better.

After all, not only has Laila got her pups back," Col. Zoro paused to fondly look at the puppies as they scampered about excitedly,

"We have also saved an important piece of our heritage. You see, this *Sultan of lead* is none other than Batuk's brother!"

"You mean the same Batuk that tried stealing the Golden Collar?" asked Captain Tipu.

"Wait, does that mean even he is…"

"Exactly Captain, he is also an **AGENT** of the Chinesc Chowchows. They wanted these pillars not for money but to stop us from proving to the world that our civilization has such a rich heritage.

After all, it is a matter of pride for any nation that their culture and heritage dates back to 7500BCE, if not more!" beamed Col. Zoro.

"The waiter who brought us Laila's message in the Ritz Canine hotel, sir," piped up Wodi.

"*Who was he*?"

"Why, it was none other than Captain Tipu, except his **disguise** was so good that even you didn't recognize him," replied Col. Zoro.

Wodi turned **red** with embarrassment.

Everyone glowed with pleasure.

The Chinese Chowchow's evil designs had been thwarted once again and one more of their villainous agents was soon going to be behind bars.

The resourceful Col. Zoro had

saved the day yet again!

Did you notice that both cases Col. Zoro's solved so far had something to do with water? The first book was about a haunted lake and the second case was about a drowned city – is that weird or what!

Thankfully, his next case takes him far away from water of any kind. Or does it?!?!?! Find out more as Col. Zoro moves from unravelling an underwater legend, to solving an underground mystery in his next case,

Abode of the Indomitables.

Books in the Det. Zoro series:

Mystery of the Haunted Lake

Abode of the Indomitables

The Comanche Connection

Mystery of the Secret Chamber

The 36th PUZZLE

Quest for the Greatest Treasure

Secret Trail of the Warrior King